Life Lessons from My Grandparents

Keen Babbage, Ed. D.

LIFE LESSONS FROM MY GRANDPARENTS

ISBN: 978-0-9982190-9-7

DEDICATION

To Keen Johnson and Eunice Johnson, truly ideal grandparents

CONTENTS

ACKNOWLEDGMENTS

The most important inspirations for this book are my maternal grandparents, Keen Johnson and Eunice Johnson. Their exemplary lives made this book possible. They also made possible much goodness which has come to our family through the years.

I also owe my mother, Judy Babbage, much gratitude. She made sure that I spent a lot of time with my grandparents. That time together, years ago, will always be a treasured gift.

My brother, Bob; my sister-in-law, Laura; my nephews, Robert and Brian; and my niece Julie, have always encouraged me in my book writing endeavors. Their kind support is essential.

Adam Turner is a masterful book publisher. After I finish word processing a manuscript and send it via e-mail to Adam, he then expertly completes a magnificent process of transforming what I typed and sent to him into a book. His creative skills, his technology skills, and his marketing skills are superior. Working with Adam on this book was Jessica Hudson whose help was vital in the process. The time, effort, and talents which she invested in this book were very productive.

INTRODUCTION

As a child I was told by a friend of my grandparents that, "It means so much to your grandparents when you visit them. They just try harder and they are so filled with energy. I can tell how much better they feel when they are with their grandchildren."

It is likely that I did not understand what I was being told. As a child I could not fully comprehend or appreciate the inspiration that grandparents receive when they are with their grandchildren.

Much understanding emerged when I watched my mother interact with, talk about, view pictures of, or look forward to being with her grandchildren. When my mother's health began to decline in her later years, the best medicine for her was to be with her grandchildren. Between visits, it was beneficial and energizing for her to talk about her grandchildren. She always smiled radiantly when she was with her grandchildren. The cares, the aches, the pains, the troubles of the day seemed to disappear whenever she was with her grandchildren.

Those grandchildren cherished Nana. Sleepovers at Nana's were delightful events with so much to do, to talk about, to play, and to discover. Some favorite foods were always available at Nana's. Books would be read aloud at Nana's. Life had an extra amount of goodness added to it when Nana and her grandchildren were together.

Because of their life experiences, and for other reasons, grandparents are a unique source of life lessons for grandchildren. This book presents some of those life lessons. The life lessons in this book are based primarily on memories of, reflections about, and thorough consideration of the treasured experiences of the author when he was a grandchild. Also, those life lessons have been confirmed and enhanced based on observations made by the author as he saw how much joy and goodness his mother brought to her grandchildren and how much joy and goodness those grandchildren brought

1

to their grandmother, known to them as Nana.

This book is not a research study on grandparents and grandchildren; rather, it is an opportunity for the author to pay loving tribute to his maternal grandparents. Also, this book is an opportunity for the reader to think about life lessons he or she has learned from his or her grandparents. The book also can be a catalyst for current grandparents to think about the life lessons which they are teaching or hope to teach to their grandchildren.

My maternal grandparents, Keen Johnson and Eunice Johnson, were exemplary people. As husband and wife, they were completely devoted to one another. I recall with abundant joy and thankfulness the celebration of their 50th wedding anniversary. There was a time during that anniversary celebration when I noticed how they looked at each other. It was as if their eyes could speak, and what their eyes communicated was pure, unlimited, true love.

My grandparents were kind, polite, caring, gracious, hospitable, friendly, wise people of faith, hope, and love. I cherish the years we shared. I value the life lessons they taught me and, through my memories of them, the life lessons that they continue to teach me.

My understanding of and my appreciation for my grandparents has increased with the passage of time. Why? Because viewed through the lens of an adult I can see my grandparents with much more thorough knowledge than I had when I was a child, a teenager, or a young adult. It is simply one of those truths of life that as we get older we gain a deeper realization of people who, when we initially knew them, were the age we are now.

As I write these words I am 64 years old. My grandparents were 64 years old when I was 6 years old. I knew that they were wonderful people when I was 6 years old. Now I understand what made them the wonderful people they were and, in my memories and thoughts, always will be.

My grandfather was born in 1896 and my grandmother was born in 1895. My brother was born in 1951 and I was born in 1954. Many years, actually, several decades passed between the births of my grandparents and the births of their grandsons. Much in our society, in our culture, in technology, in media, in economics, in politics, and in other aspects of how people live changed during those years and decades.

Yet, as I have become the age my grandparents were when I was a child, it has become precisely clear to me that some aspects of life should not change. What matters most – such as love, family, caring, being together, faith, hope, and friendship among other forever vital human values and virtues – are some of the parts of life which are timeless.

My grandparents understood what matters most and they followed the standard of doing what matters most. I saw them live that way. Decades later I realize how wise, how honorable, how everlasting, how permanent their understanding of what matters most in life was. To know what matters most and to live accordingly is a priceless life lesson which my grandparents continue to teach me as I remember and reflect upon their exemplary lives.

The life lessons from my grandparents which are presented in this book are timeless. No doubt, there are more life lessons from grandparents than the lessons which are included in this book. The reader of any age is encouraged to think of life lessons which he or she has learned from grandparents. The reader who is a grandparent is encouraged to think of the life lessons which he or she has taught, is teaching, or would like to teach to his or her grandchildren.

In addition to sharing ideas with and inspiring ideas within readers, there are two very personal reasons for writing this book. One, this book is a way for me to pay tribute to my grandparents. Two, this book is a way for my niece and my nephews to know more about the grandparents of their father and of their uncle. My niece and nephews did not get to meet their great-grandparents, but they have heard much about them. With this book, I hope they will more fully know the dear people to whom this book is dedicated: my grandparents, their great-grandparents.

Grandchildren often use a term of endearment or a family nickname for their grandparents. We called our grandmother "Muny" and we called our grandfather "Paw-Wah." The precise origins of those fondly used names are not known.

I had a serious speech impediment as a child and as a teenager, so perhaps Muny was the closest I could get to saying grandmother. Maybe I heard the word Grandpa and Paw-Wah was the best I could do to pronounce that. The nicknames may have been established by my parents and my older brother. The source is simply not known. The connection between grandparent and grandchild which those names confirmed is very well known and is fondly remembered. The nicknames were accepted by the family, including my grandparents, and became part of the bond we shared.

Let us now celebrate grandparents and the life lessons which they teach us.

Keen Babbage, Ed. D.
Lexington, Kentucky
March 2019

KEEN BABBAGE, ED.D.

1
LOVE

It would be quite accurate if a dictionary had as one of the definitions for "love" these words: "what the best grandmothers and grandfathers abundantly give their grandchildren." A grandmother's love for her grandchildren or a grandfather's love for his grandchildren has a unique wonder, beauty, and meaning. How is that possible?

The love a grandparent has for a grandchild is double love. I know how deeply my grandparents loved my mother. They were dedicated to her and they cherished her. I know how equally deeply my mother loved her parents. She was dedicated to them and she cherished them.

When my older brother Bob and I were each born, our parents loved us immediately and always would love us. When Bob and I were born, our grandparents loved us immediately and always would love us. Our grandparents loved our parents and our grandparents loved my brother and me. That is double love. That is one characteristic of the unique love which I recall my grandparents had for their grandchildren.

My grandparents were always thrilled to be with their grandchildren. Upon arriving at the house where my grandparents lived, we were always greeted with smiles, hugs, and joy. We knew they were glad to see us. The pleasure my grandparents experienced when we arrived was contagious and helped create an atmosphere where everyone was encouraged, uplifted, and important.

The unlimited love my grandparents shared with me showed that I mattered to my grandparents. As a child and as a teenager, it was very good to know that being with me was quite important to and was very meaningful for my grandparents. Their joy in being with me taught me the life lesson of expressing love for people who you care about, beginning with your family.

When we would arrive at my grandparents' house, one or both of them would greet us at the door. We could have opened the door ourselves. We could have knocked on the door or sounded the doorbell. No, that would not do, because part of the vast expression of love which Muny and Paw-Wah showed began at the very moment of our arrival at their home.

How can something as simple as being at the door to welcome someone when they arrive be part of showing love? It is an extra effort which communicates, "I am so glad to see you. I am so thankful that you are here. Every moment we are together is important to me."

When a visit with my grandparents ended, one or both of them would walk with us to the door and sometimes to our car. What did this communicate? "It was wonderful to be with you. We want to extend this visit to the very moment when you drive away. We eagerly anticipate your next visit. We are very thankful for you. We love you, a lot."

Between the welcome at the door and the conclusion of a visit, the time with my grandparents was filled with shared activities that captivated me. My grandmother would go out of her way to plan a perfect meal for us. My grandfather would read a story to me. My grandmother would tell me about her experiences as a child in Missouri. My grandfather would tell me about the challenges he faced as a soldier during World War I. My grandmother would show me pictures of relatives I had not met. My grandfather and I would play Checkers.

Those shared experiences were not expensive. Those shared times were genuine. Those shared times created memories which are forever treasured. Those shared times communicated to me, "Of all the places I could be and of all the people I could be with, nothing means more to me than to be with you, right now, right here." Sharing of uninterrupted time taught me the life lesson that when we make being with another person a priority that nothing can interfere with, we show that person that we lovingly value him or her.

I recall watching my grandparents sometimes. I would not stare because that is impolite, but I would observe and realize that something was going on. My grandparents would look at each other with a shared expression of love and devotion which a child could notice. No words had to be spoken for their love to be communicated. That love and devotion built the foundation of their "until death do us part" dedication to each other. Seeing that commitment based on love taught me that one part of being family is that we love each other.

I knew that being with me was important to my grandparents. That certainty gave me much encouragement and assurance as I grew through childhood and through the teenage years. I may have noticed as a child, but I certainly realize it now, that I was not the most important person in my grandmother's life or in my grandfather's life. For my grandparents, they were the most important person in each other's life. Their absolute devotion to each other was a life-long fulfillment of their wedding vows and of their understanding of love between a husband and a wife.

Related to what I learned from my grandparents about their dedication to each other was this scene which I saw many, many times. In my grandparents' home there was a spacious living room. They spent much of their time each day in that room. When we visited my grandparents, the living room was the place where we would gather to talk, to read, to share with each other what we were reading, and to watch the news on television.

Whenever my grandparents were in the living room, and my grandfather needed to leave the living room, he would walk over to my grandmother and gently kiss her on the forehead. I never asked why he did that or what it meant for him to do that. It was obvious that this was another way that my grandparents expressed their love for each other. It also was part of my grandfather's exemplary behavior as a gentleman. Even as a child, it seemed to me that what I was watching revealed an important life lesson – each moment is an opportunity to show the people you love, that you love them. Those opportunities should be acted upon sincerely, genuinely, and properly.

It is interesting to think that sometimes Muny and Paw-Wah were teaching me life lessons when they were simply and genuinely living the moment-to-moment activities of their lives. My grandfather did not say, "Keen, watch this and notice how I acknowledge your grandmother before I step out of the living room." His action spoke so loudly that no words were needed. His action toward my grandmother was not designed to teach me, although it certainly did; rather, his action was authentically showing his bride that he forever treasured her, revered her, loved her and that he highly valued the life they shared as a couple.

My grandparents were part of the generation which reared the people whom Tom Brokaw described in his literary masterpiece as "The Greatest Generation." The members of "The Greatest Generation" were the people who boldly responded to the needs of the United States during World War II. What made "The Greatest Generation" members so filled with a love of country, with an unsurpassed work ethic, with a sense of patriotism, with a can-do attitude, and with unlimited concern about their families?

One answer to the question of "What made The Greatest Generation" the people they were is the parents and extended family members who reared them. My grandparents reflected the eternal truths which they had been taught by their families and which they taught to their family: integrity, honor, work ethic, commitment, civic concern, honesty, service to your country, devotion to your family, and endless love for your family. "The Greatest Generation" was made possible by the prior generation which my grandparents were part of and which can continue to teach us today.

My great-grandmother had health difficulties for many years as she aged. She was hospitalized for a very long time. My grandmother visited her mother

- my great-grandmother – each day during that long hospital stay. Nothing could prevent my grandmother from going to the hospital and visiting her mother daily. With her endless acts of kindness to and concern for her mother, Muny showed us what love looks like.

When I visited my grandparents during that lengthy period of my great-grandmother's hospitalization, there would be a time in the afternoon, each afternoon, any afternoon, every afternoon when my grandmother would go to the hospital to visit her mother. My grandmother lovingly visited her hospitalized mother every day regardless of any other plans, responsibilities, or time commitments my grandmother had. I noticed as a child how steadfast my grandmother was in this devotion to her mother. What I noticed and what I forever remember was kindness in action, compassion in action, and love in action.

The drive from my grandparent's house in Richmond, Kentucky to the house where we lived in Lexington, Kentucky took about 30 minutes. More often than not, as we walked into our house upon returning from a visit, the phone would be ringing. We knew who was calling. My grandmother was checking to be sure that we arrived home safely. As a child, I wondered then if those calls were necessary. Now I know that yes, they were necessary because my grandmother's love for us included those calls to assure herself that her family was safe and to show us that her concern for us was continuous. Those calls also showed caring and love.

During his career, my grandfather became very involved in politics and then he worked in public relations for a large company, but before both of those endeavors, he was a very accomplished and very respected journalist. He read newspapers daily and he read weekly news magazines. He would make the effort to encourage me to read those publications. Then, he would answer my questions about what I had read.

There were many other possible uses of his time, but he invested time in me so I could understand events which were in the news. The news topics were important. The time we shared discussing those news topics was more important. As I reflect upon those conversations, I realize that sharing time together in wholesome ways is another way to express love.

When I was eight years old, the family gathered at my grandparents' home for Christmas Eve. Everyone was seated at the dining room table for supper. My great-grandmother, my grandparents, my parents, my brother, and I were joined in a time of being thankful, being aware of the true meaning of the holy day that would follow, and of being filled with the goodness that comes from being together for such an occasion.

Before an absolutely perfect meal of traditional home cooking that was unsurpassed, my grandfather presented my grandmother with a gift. The gift was wrapped quite artistically. I noticed that the present was quite small, but that my grandmother was filled with anticipation as she unwrapped the gift and then opened the box which the wrapping paper had covered.

Moments later my grandmother was crying. I said to my mother, "Doesn't she like her present?" My mother explained, that my grandmother was overjoyed with her present and that the tears expressed delight which words could not communicate. No doubt, to my way of thinking as a child, I found that explanation to be confusing. In later years, that explanation would make perfect sense to me. There are times when tears say what words cannot.

The gift was a very attractive piece of jewelry which my grandfather had selected personally and precisely for the dear woman who was the forever love of his life. As a child, I continued to connect crying with sadness. Later in life, I would understand that there can be tears of gladness. Later in life, I would realize how filled with joy my grandmother was at the moment she opened that gift. Later in life, I would realize how filled with love the marriage of my grandparents was from the day of their wedding until death did they part.

Further refection, 56 years after that memorable Christmas Eve, about that moment tells me that it was not the attractive piece of jewelry in the box which brought tears of gladness to my grandmother's eyes.

Yes, she liked the jewelry very much. Yes, she would wear that piece of jewelry with much pleasure. However, the gift in the box was not the cause of the tears. What was the cause? It was the abundant love in my grandfather's heart which, as had been done for decades, was being given to my grandmother. Her tears of gladness provided a way for her to lovingly respond to her husband. What might have seemed to me as merely being one Christmas present was truly part of the gift my grandparents shared for a lifetime: love that grew, love that knew no limits, love that showed what mattered most, but that also showed who mattered most. That is a lesson about life, about love, and about priorities.

There is another life lesson which can be learned from that Christmas Eve moment: I was not the center of attention at the dining room table. There was an element of seniority earned by my grandparents and that seniority deserved complete respect. There was an element of deference that was owed to my grandparents.

It is realistic to say that chronologically and in other vital ways my grandparents had made our family possible. All the love that everyone at that dining room table on Christmas Eve felt for my grandparents was genuine. Part of the love that everyone at that dining room table on Christmas Eve felt for my grandparents was based on the fact that those two beloved people were worthy of honor, respect, gratitude, and love itself.

At the young age of 14, I started developing an interest in becoming a teacher. My grandfather and I discussed this possible career path. His very productive and very impressive career had been in journalism, politics, and public relations. He did not direct me toward following into the work he had done. Instead, he encouraged my interest in becoming a teacher. He told me it would be important to continue to read a lot and to read a variety of sources including newspapers, news magazines, history books, biographies, and more.

Throughout my 34 years of work as a teacher and as a school administrator, I occasionally thought of the encouraging conversations I had with my grandfather about my career interest. During difficult times in my career, I found inspiration from my grandfather's certainty that I would be a very good teacher.

Fifty years after those conversations, my grandfather's kind, caring, loving words of support continue to guide me and to invigorate me. Fifty years after those conversations were shared in the living room of my grandparents' home, I continue to hear my grandfather's words. Fifty years after those conversations, I continue to benefit from the many life lessons taught to me by my grandparents, dearly known as Muny and Paw-Wah.

My grandfather took the time to listen to me. The time he invested in me inspired results in my career as an educator which have been obtained throughout several decades. He loved me enough to care, to advise, to support, and to encourage. Part of my determination to get high quality results in my work as an educator has been that those results are a way for me to say thank you to my grandfather for the career support he gave to me as part of the love a grandparent gives to a grandchild.

Consider these sacred words: "Love is patient, love is kind. It does not envy, it does not boast, it is not proud. It is not rude, it is not self-seeking, it is not easily angered, it keeps no record of wrongs. Love does not delight in evil, but rejoices in the truth. It always protects, always trusts, always hopes, always perseveres. Love never fails…" (1 Corinthians 13: 4-8; New International Version of the Bible).

Knowing about the childhood life experiences and the teenage life experiences of my grandparents, I can be assured that they heard those words from the Bible read at their homes, taught to them by their families, and taught to them at their churches. Knowing the people whom my grandparents became during their adult years and knowing the example they set for me, I am certain that they lived by those words.

The first and the most important life lesson which my grandparents taught me, by their words and by their actions, is love. How wise they were to establish that as the guiding priority, as the overall priority, as the forever priority.

2
FAMILY, HOLIDAYS, AND MEALS

"We are a small family. We have to pull for each other." Since my grandfather spoke those words to my brother and me in the year 1966, when I was 12 years old, I have been inspired by the wisdom expressed in those two sentences. Whether a family is large or small, family members need to "pull for each other" and, as my grandfather perceived, in a small family the need to "pull for each other" is of extra importance.

My grandfather's choice of verb in the second sentence of his wise statement has intrigued me for decades. When he spoke those words originally, I was somewhat perplexed about how it would be possible for one person to pull for another person, but I sensed that it must mean something about helping each other. In the decades since those words were spoken, deeper meanings and more precise meanings have become quite clear.

Yes, to pull for someone does mean to help them. My grandfather was giving us a family directive that we were to help each other always. He was also giving us part of himself, part of his life experience, part of what he had learned from his family experiences, and part of what he knew to be true, essential, and good.

My grandfather's father was a Methodist circuit-riding minister in western Kentucky. Income for a person in that line of work at that time was very limited, but the family endured. Sacrifices were made, priorities were set, budgets were tight, rules were clear, and family commitments were strong. No doubt, my grandfather learned the importance of family members pulling for each other from his parents.

When I was a sophomore in college, the first semester had ended, but I was going to stay on campus for an additional two days to watch some college basketball games. On the evening of the day that final exams had ended, there

11

was a phone call for me. This was in the days when there was one telephone per floor of the dormitory and there were no cell phones. I answered the phone politely and immediately heard my grandmother's voice.

I shared with her some news about my classes and my final exams. She then said, "Now, your mother needs you to be at home with her during this Christmas time. You have finished the semester, so do not delay in getting home." There was only one acceptable response to my grandmother's instruction. I said, "Yes, ma'am." I did not stay for the basketball games. I drove home early the next morning.

My grandmother's call pulled me away from the college campus to our home. That might not have been exactly what my grandfather was thinking of when he said, "We have to pull for each other," yet, upon further reflection, it is an exact example of what he meant. I was needed at home. The basketball games would function well without me. My family and I would function better with me at home for all of the holiday season and the time between semesters.

No person would notice my absence from the basketball games. My mother and my grandmother would notice my absence from home, even if only for a day or two. Going home was the right action to take. My grandmother understood that, and I soon learned that her guidance was based on making family the priority it should be.

My mother and my grandparents spoke by phone daily. It was usually a short conversation, but its importance was not measured according to the length of the phone call; rather, being in touch was what mattered. There might be some news of the day to share. Perhaps my brother and/or I had accomplished something at school and my grandparents would be interested in that. Plans for a family visit could be discussed. Sometimes ideas were traded, decisions were made, or advice was given. The phone at our home would ring daily on weekdays and often on the weekends. The phone would ring at about 4:30 p.m. and we knew it was my grandmother who was calling. The certainty of that daily phone call was reassuring.

If my brother was at home and/or if I was at home when that daily phone call occurred, we would usually enter the conversation. Our grandparents were delighted to hear our voices. I did not fully understand or appreciate how important it was to them that they talked often with their daughter and with their grandsons, but I knew that the phone calls were pleasant and were eagerly anticipated. It is quite likely that those phone calls were one of the brightest parts of each day for my grandparents. Keeping in touch was quite important to our family and, as I think about it now, those phone calls were one way that we could "pull for each other."

Those same phone calls did not occur always on the weekends because that was often a time to visit our grandparents. A typical weekend at our home would include chores to do around the house, playing with friends in the neighborhood, school work to complete, social events our parents attended which meant a dear family friend would babysit for my brother and me, and going to church on Sunday.

Weekends were at their best when a visit with Muny and Paw-Wah was included. These visits were not reserved only for holidays or other special occasions; rather, each of the visits themselves always became a special occasion. My grandmother would plan a meal that no restaurant could equal. The food was not fancy; instead, the food was the most delicious and memorable down-home cooking possible.

Meals were served in the dining room. This was in an era before anything handheld, electronic, or digital existed, but if those devices had existed then, they would be far away from the dining room during a meal. The food was always perfect, but the food was only one reason that dining together was such a significant and heart-warming time. These meals provided a time when everyone concentrated on the goodness of and the gift of being together. We raved about the food, but the food was a helpful supporting member of the cast of the event. The people and the sharing of time together were the true stars of these gatherings.

We prayed before the meal was served. Everyone received their food before anyone could begin eating. When food was passed from person to person there were many "thank you" and "please" comments. There was much discussion. There were smiles and laughs. There were corrections given to my brother and/or to me if we strayed from proper dining room manners and behavior. When the meal ended, everyone helped with clearing the table and with other work that needed to be done. Meals were a shared experience and the sharing made each meal a meaningful experience. And, yes, the food was absolutely outstanding.

Celebrating holidays at my grandparents' home meant that each holiday was ideal. Thanksgiving, Christmas, and Easter were given the most attention. Birthdays became another version of a holiday. We were always reminded by our grandparents about the real meaning of each holiday that had a sacred origin.

There were traditions that we followed. Our Thanksgiving meal always began with prayer and then included turkey, dressing, mashed potatoes, gravy, cranberries, and rolls which were freshly baked in the kitchen. Christmas included reading scripture and then giving gifts to each other. Easter included going to church and then a hunt for Easter eggs.

The traditions were one reason that as a child I eagerly awaited each holiday. My grandparents made sure that I understood in addition to the good traditions, there were other parts of each holiday that must not be overshadowed by those traditions. We were taught and re-taught what Thanksgiving was about, what Christmas was about, and what Easter was about.

More than half a century since those holidays were shared with my grandparents during my childhood, I can picture in my mind those perfect meals with such detail that it is as if I am being served the meal again at this moment. In a wonderful way, I am being served those meals again because the memory of those meals is a reminder of precious family times.

More than the meals, I can recall the lessons we were taught about the importance of each holiday and of the reason for each holiday. I remember that our family prayed before each meal. I remember that we made sure that everyone received what they needed. We took care of each other. In the seemingly ordinary moment-to-moment actions of daily life, we expressed our devotion to each other.

My grandparents knew how to turn family time, holidays, and meals into gifts which made those shared times some of the best times anyone could experience, and which have provided a lifetime of prized memories. With each memory of those family times together, I smile, and I give thanks. I am inspired, and I am encouraged. I am loved anew, and I express love anew as I also give thanks.

There were some simpler meals which I shared with my grandparents. They had a small "breakfast room" at their home between the kitchen and the dining room. The breakfast menu was less elaborate than the dining room meals, but the food was always excellent. No family member ate alone in the breakfast room. Meals were to be shared. Time was to be shared. The food was quite good, yet the time together was even better. Combining the good food and the shared time added to the quality of the day for everyone.

My brother and I were eating breakfast with my grandfather one morning. My grandmother had prepared a splendid meal of orange juice, grapefruit, scrambled eggs, bacon, sausage, toast with jam, jelly, butter, or honey. My grandfather was telling us about an article he had read in the morning paper. We listened with much interest as he explained how a certain political process worked.

I then heard my grandmother express some disappointment in and dissatisfaction with the breakfast she had prepared for and served to us. "I used to think I was a good breakfast cook," she lamented with the implication that she could no longer fix the meal up to her standards. My grandfather immediately replied, "You are a wonderful breakfast cook." He then lovingly looked at her and she lovingly looked at him. His words and his expression had reassured my grandmother that her ability to prepare a very good breakfast was intact. No more words had to be spoken. My grandmother's smile showed that all was well.

There is a life lesson to be learned from that exchange between Muny and Paw-Wah. It is important for people to be appreciated. It is important also for people to be cheered, to be comforted, and to be assured of their worth. Family members need to do that for each other. Everyone benefits when appreciation, cheering, and assurance are offered and received. The person offering the kindness knows that his or her caring action is the right thing to do. The person receiving the kindness regains confidence in and certainty about herself or himself.

Reflecting from the perspective of a 64-year-old, I can realize more now than I could as a child. When my grandfather expressed appreciation and assurance to my grandmother, he was showing that the most important commitment in his life was to his wife. My grandparents were ideal parents and grandparents, yet above all they were completely devoted to each other as husband and wife. It was that original devotion to each other that became the foundation for their dedication to their daughter and then to their grandsons.

How much time does it take to offer appreciation to another family member? Very little time. How much effort does it take to offer appreciation to another family member? Not much. What is needed to make sure that we offer appreciation? Awareness of and sensitivity to the needs of another person, followed by proper action which helps meet those needs.

What types of actions? Perhaps a few words will be sufficient. A caring moment of eye contact can help. A hug could be necessary. Those kind acts can occur whenever we make the effort which is very good news because it means that there is no limit on expressions of kindness if only we will take action properly.

My grandfather and I played many games of Checkers. Each of us played to win and the results would show that each of us had our share of victories and of losses. Viewed differently, there were no losses. Of course, in each game one player got to the point where he had no moves left or no Checkers pieces left, so that game ended, and the next game would begin.

I recall no sadness or frustration when I lost a game of Checkers while playing that game with my grandfather. I do recall the smiles we shared as we played Checkers, as we talked about the game, as we evaluated possible moves, and as we thought about the best next move to make. I am sure that I did my best to win as often as I could. I am also sure that my grandfather did his best to win as often as he could. The competition was genuine. Yet, the competition is not what I remember most.

What is remembered is my grandfather, sitting in his favorite wing-back chair, the Checkers board resting on the ottoman in front of the chair, and I was sitting on the floor by the ottoman. I remember that there was no mention of time, no mention of anything else that needed to be done, and no reference to any schedule that would bring an end to the Checkers games.

I know now that my grandfather had other uses of his time, but I deeply value now that he shared that time with me. The time we spent playing Checkers was very enjoyable. The memories of those Checkers games make me smile 55 years later. Playing Checkers together, and sharing other wholesome activities together, that's just part of what families should do according to the good example I saw when I was a child.

My grandparents liked the card game Bridge. As a child I did not understand that game, but I was intrigued by it and curious about it. When I visited my grandparents and Bridge was played at their home, perhaps with my parents or with friends of my grandparents, I was allowed to sit near the card table and listen to the bidding and then to the comments as each hand was played.

I would occasionally ask a question and I would be given a quick answer, but I would be reminded that I needed to politely – that meant silently – listen and watch. I was eager to know what the red cards stood for and what the black cards stood for and what did the bids mean. What language was "2 Hearts" or "3 Clubs"? I learned to be quiet, to watch attentively because by doing that I would get to stay with the grown-ups.

Bridge playing was something that grown-ups got to do, but by being allowed to watch and listen I felt a part of the grown-up Bridge game. I looked forward to the time when I would learn how to play Bridge because if that game was something my grandparents enjoyed playing together with my parents or with friends, I wanted to find a way to be more involved.

I could have been told to go into another room and play or read, but I was allowed to be with my family as they played Bridge. I learned to be silent during Bridge games and to save my questions for after the game ended. My family established rules for proper behavior and by doing that they made the effort to include me. That shared time is a very valuable gift that families can give.

There are common threads that run through the topics of family, holidays, and meals. These include being together and really interacting together, sharing time together in pleasant ways, keeping in touch, making an extra effort so special occasions are just as they should be, expressing concern for one another, showing each family member that they are noticed and cared for and valued.

There is one more thread that runs through family, holidays, and meals. That thread is that, "We have to pull for each other." When family members "pull for each other" consistently and in wholesome ways, family bonds are strengthened, grow deeper, and touch lives in ways that endure forever. There is much wisdom in the statement, "We have to pull for each other." There is much goodness that can be accomplished and shared when the wisdom of that statement is implemented through wholesome actions by families.

3
FRIENDS AND HOSPITALITY

The lovely house which was my grandparent's home had a staircase which, at its first floor base, intersected with the entry hallway of the home, opposite the front door. Put another way, upon entering the front door, their living room was to the right, their dining room was to the left, and the staircase was straight ahead. To a child it was a magnificent setting. More than that, the staircase provided a perfect place to stay during the frequent times when friends of my grandparents would visit.

My brother and I would sit on stairs and listen to the conversations which were occurring around the corner in the living room. When people visited my grandfather, the main topic was usually politics, including elections, bills being considered by the Kentucky legislature when they were in session, and events in Washington, D.C. Other frequent topics included higher education, the Kentucky Derby, golf, and current news events.

Listening to those conversations provided an unequaled education. Our vocabulary grew as we heard clearly chosen and very impressive words which expressed important ideas. Our curiosity about, awareness of, and understanding of the topics which were discussed increased. We were always glad whenever friends of our grandparents would stop by so we could meet these dear people and so we could hear the conversations which to us were very sophisticated and which we hoped someday we would be knowledgeable enough to participate in.

Friends who visited my grandparents were always treated with perfect, gracious, and sincere hospitality. I recall that there were many smiles shared whenever visitors arrived. My grandparents would genuinely and eagerly welcome guests. It seemed to me that each visit was a big event because there was such excitement and delight when visitors arrived. I began to notice that the welcome greeting from my grandparents to their visitors did not vary; rather, it was always very friendly and always very sincere.

Upon reflection, I can realize that Muny and Paw-Wah knew many people, had many close friends, and graciously welcomed every visitor. The cordial greetings as people entered the home were followed by everyone going into the living room. Sometimes there would be one big conversation. Then, two conversations could emerge as the ladies had their discussion and the gentlemen had their discussion. Friendship and hospitality combined to create much shared enjoyment for my grandparents and their visitors.

While those conversations were taking place, my brother and I would carefully listen. We especially were interested in discussions my grandfather had about politics. From a very young age, we had heard discussions about government, about elections, about candidates, and who would likely win. No doubt, those stairway learning sessions had an impact on my brother who had much success in his political career and on me as during my teaching career I usually taught Political Science or United States History.

There was a lesson learned whenever it became time for the guests to leave. I remember hearing most visitors say that they would return as soon as possible. That sincere promise pleased my grandparents. They anticipated the next visit with much eagerness. It became apparent to me that having friendships was an important part of living well.

As a child and as a teenager, I was fortunate to have many friends from school, from our neighborhood, and from church. My grandparents would occasionally ask me about my friends, by name. I had the opportunity to meet some of my grandparents' friends. The lesson emerged that friendships are important at any age, at every age.

My grandparents knew so much about creating an atmosphere of hospitality and did so much to create an atmosphere of hospitality at their home, that they deserve to be called experts on the topic. When friends arrived at their home, my grandparents would offer them something to drink, which usually meant water or iced tea. The beverage would be served in an attractive glass which would sit on a coaster. Using a coaster was wise for protection of furniture, while it also added a touch of stylish hospitality. As a child I could understand that a coaster was useful, but I could also sense that it was polite, proper, and hospitable.

I kept some of the coasters which my grandparents used at their home. These coasters have endured many decades. They remind me of the example I saw of people making an extra effort to provide every detail of making people welcome, of graciousness, of hospitality.

My grandmother had a fondness for a certain type of candy which came from a local, family owned and operated, very traditional candy store in Lexington, Kentucky. Her favorite candy was a soft, melt-in-your mouth mint which came in various colors which carried various flavors. She would very politely pass a plate of these candies to guests. Most people gladly accepted a piece of this handmade candy. Of course, second servings were offered.

Is it a requirement to offer a guest a piece of candy? No. Does a guest appreciate being offered a piece of candy? Yes. My grandmother knew that and acted accordingly. As I think about those wonderful years in the deeply valued past, it has become clear to me that my grandmother always offered beverages and candy, or some snack, to guests. It was done out of friendship and hospitality. She knew of no other way to treat guests than to be very gracious. More importantly, it was what my grandmother expected of herself. There was no option and there was no alternative.

A friend of my grandparents was always invited to join our family for Thanksgiving. She lived alone a few houses away from my grandparents. Everyone enjoyed having her with us. She always brought a homemade jam cake. Was that required? No, of course not. There was no requirement or expectation that an invited guest had to bring anything. Yet, I am certain that she found much satisfaction in baking the flavorful cake and in sharing it with us.

Perhaps it was an expression of reciprocal hospitality. My great-grandmother, my grandparents, my parents, my brother and I were pleased to share the holiday with a close family friend. It meant a lot to us that she joined us so we could be together, enjoy friendship, and extend mutual hospitality. Those acts of kindness made an impression on me and taught a life lesson: at every opportunity, strengthen friendships by offering hospitality and by expressing thoughtful, real acts of kindness.

My grandparents had a deep fondness for Kentucky. My grandmother was from Missouri, but she lived all of her adult life in Kentucky. My grandfather was from Kentucky and lived all of his adult life in the Bluegrass State. One of the grand traditions in Kentucky, one of the most well-known features of Kentucky, is high quality thoroughbred horse racing. My grandparents greatly enjoyed going to the Keeneland race track in Lexington and to the Kentucky Derby in Louisville.

There were many times when our entire family went to the horse races together. These were very proper events and dressing up was required. I recall the excitement of the horse races. I remember the unique foods served at the racing tracks. Although much attention is on the horses, as much or more attention is on the people who are there.

As a child it seemed to me that my grandparents knew everyone at Keeneland. The people who managed the dining facility always welcomed our family with much hospitality. That way of treating people is part of the Keeneland tradition. My grandparents would speak to those very polite workers by name and the workers would call my grandparents by name.

It fascinated me that everyone knew each other's name. How did that happen? It happened because knowing a person's name and speaking to them accordingly was part of the tradition of hospitality which my grandparents lived by and which Keeneland is known for.

Throughout a day at Keeneland, many people would stop by the lunch table where our family ate. We always sat at the same table. It was close to a major doorway which led to the betting windows and to an excellent view of the horse races.

Never were there so many pauses in a meal as there would be at Keeneland. Friends of my grandparents knew where they would be sitting for lunch on a Saturday during the Spring or the Fall racing meets at Keeneland. Those friends would stop for a cordial conversation. There were many smiles as everyone benefitted from visiting together.

After finishing lunch, we would go to our reserved seats outside to watch the horse races. Again, the day would be filled with friends of my grandparents coming to our area of seats and spending time to talk, to visit, to be together. There were more smiles. There were also some conversations which caught my attention. Would a new constitution for Kentucky be approved by the voters? Who would win an upcoming election?

Throughout all of these visits and conversations there was a constant expression of friendship. These visits were not a quick, "Hi. How are you?" Rather, they were updates of connections and commitments between people who truly valued each other, who had worked together for many years, who had socialized together often, and who just enjoyed one another's company. The horses were exciting to watch. The people and their visits were fascinating to watch.

Upon reflection, it becomes clear that people at the horse racing events spent two minutes at various times throughout the day watching the horses race. People spent hours throughout the day interacting with each other. The horse races attracted the people in the crowd to attend the event. The people in the crowd attracted each other as friendships began, as friendships grew, as hospitality was abundant.

The same emphasis was noticed at the Kentucky Derby. This is one of the most magnificent of all sporting events. People from throughout the United States and throughout the world attend the Kentucky Derby. It is a two-minute horse race that is unsurpassed in thrills, in celebration, in captivating an audience, and in putting the spotlight on Kentucky. When "My Old Kentucky Home" is sung, 160,000 people in attendance at Churchill Downs share a few moments of unity, ceremony, tribute, and thankfulness.

As a child, I attended the Kentucky Derby with my brother, my parents, and my grandparents twice. The memories are vivid. The memories of what? Horses, of course, especially in a close race. The memories of people stand out even more. As at Keeneland, it seemed as if my grandparents knew everyone at the Derby. As a child I may have wondered if horse racing events, unlike any other sporting event, brought out a unique energy in people.

Enthusiasts of other sporting events could claim the uniqueness of their chosen activities. What I know about going to Keeneland and to the Kentucky Derby with my family was that these were eagerly anticipated and very pleasantly experienced family events. I also know that at Keeneland and at the Kentucky Derby I saw friendships in action. These family activities strengthened my awareness that friendships really matter, that friendships are a great gift people can give to each other, and that friendships deserve to be nurtured.

As age had an impact on the energy, mobility, and overall health of my grandfather, he needed some new help and support. Most of that assistance came from our family. We had more frequent weekend visits. My mother visited her parents during the week more often. This was at a time prior to the common availability of home health care, nursing homes or senior citizen living communities.

Another person was a big help to my grandfather. This gentleman came to my grandparents' home each weekday morning to help my grandfather with the morning routine of shaving, getting dressed, and going to the living room to begin reading the day's newspapers. The times I was there when the gentleman was helping are filled with memories of much conversation coming from the room where my grandfather was getting ready for the day.

My grandfather and the gentleman were from different backgrounds, were of two different generations, and had few similar life experiences; yet, they formed a friendship. The pay was fair, and the daily work time was short, but something was occurring that transcended pay and hours. My grandfather and the gentleman became friends.

They discussed their families, their churches, politics, and other topics. They laughed often. This friendship was a needed source of encouragement to my grandfather. This friendship also provided a mentor's guidance to the gentleman who was helping. The gentleman did not do this work merely for the monetary pay. He was earning more than money. My grandfather did not regret having this financial expense. He was paying for a gift which he daily gave himself. This gift was mutually beneficial as friendship grew daily.

The gentleman who helped my grandfather could have gone through the motions of assisting so that he merely provided functional support. He went far beyond that. He talked with my grandfather. He encouraged my grandfather. He helped make it possible for my grandfather to be more active than he otherwise would have been.

He helped my grandmother who knew that her husband was cared for in a very proper and favorable way. In the process of doing simple tasks, a friendship emerged. That is a reminder that friendship can occur in places and in ways that are not always the most obvious or the most expected. That insight into friendship provides another life lesson from my grandparents.

4

FAITH AND HOPE

My grandparents were people of faith. They believed in each other. They believed in their marriage. They believed that their commitment to each other was "until death do you part." They believed that their marital devotion was the foundation of their family devotion. Keen Johnson and Eunice Johnson believed that sharing life with each other was exactly the way that the two of them were intended to live.

They believed that they would become parents, and, in time, they did. They believed that having a child was a sacred responsibility and a holy blessing. They believed that providing a good life for their daughter was the honorable duty of conscientious parents. They believed that sharing life with each other and with their daughter was life at its best.

They believed in being polite, in being honest, in hard work, in honor, in being of service to the community, in appreciating friends, in providing hospitality, in carefully managing money, and in making a difference for good in the lives of other people.

They believed in education and made sure that their daughter and their grandchildren were very well educated. They believed in continuing to learn throughout their lives, so they read newspapers, news magazines, and books as part of their daily routine.

They believed in Kentucky, which was their home for many decades. They believed in the goodness of Kentucky's people, in the importance of Kentucky's history, and in the many reasons to call Kentucky home.

Muny and Paw-Wah believed in God. They took the Christian faith seriously. They prayed before each meal. They attended church and supported their churches. They strongly believed in Christianity, yet they also believed in honoring their faith heritage. My grandfather, the son of a

Methodist circuit-riding minister, attended the Methodist church throughout his life. My grandmother attended the Christian (Disciples of Christ) Church throughout her life.

The original source of the following idea is not known, but I have a bookmark which, in my grandmother's handwriting, has these words about the gospels of the New Testament in the Christian Bible written on it: "Matthew caught the authenticity of Jesus; Mark caught the power of Jesus; Luke caught the compassion of Jesus; John caught the depth of Jesus." My grandmother read those gospels and believed what they taught her.

In a speech my grandfather presented at the 1940 Kentucky Methodist Church Conference he stated, "Yet with it all I do thank God that I was reared in a Methodist parsonage; that I was reared by godly parents; that reverence for religion was inculcated in me. I am certain that such traits of character as I may possess are the result of that environment." (Public Papers of Governor Keen Johnson; published in 1982 by the University Press of Kentucky; page 438)

My grandparents were married in 1917, the same year that my grandfather began service in the armed forces of the United States. He served during World War I in France. It took much faith and much hope to get married at that time, in those turbulent national and international conditions, and as my grandfather began his military service. My grandparents were people of faith and hope.

My grandparents had a sincere hope for the community which they called home. I recall a town hall meeting my grandfather attended. The topic was whether an important connector street in their city should be widened. Most people at the meeting were adamantly against the idea of investing the money and authorizing the work to widen the road.

My grandfather presented a strong case for widening the road. He knew that the city was growing. He knew that the connector street between the downtown area and a regional university would have an ongoing increase in traffic for many years to come. His foresight was precise. In years and decades that followed the amount of traffic on that road grew, but the proposal for extra road lanes, which my grandfather said would be needed, was rejected.

When he arrived home from that meeting my grandmother asked him how the meeting had gone. He responded to her that the people at the meeting would not tolerate a few months of construction-caused inconvenience for decades of more efficient traffic flow. His words were to this effect: "They didn't see the future." He did see the future and the future with increased traffic unfolded as he had anticipated it. Eventually, road changes were made.

That disappointment did not eliminate or reduce the hope my grandparents had for their community or the faith they had in their community. They valued the many friendships they had in their town. They had a wonderful neighborhood where people eagerly helped one another.

As a child I was impressed that my grandparents' neighbors were always so glad to see each other and that neighbors invited each other for visits and for meals. There was a shared appreciation for one another and a shared sense that each person in the neighborhood had a responsibility to help everyone else, to be polite to everyone else, to be thoughtful toward everyone else.

My grandparents had abundant hopes for my brother and for me. When he was a junior in high school, my brother decided to run in a school-wide election for president of the school's Student Council. He mentioned this to my grandfather who replied, "We will get some campaign cards printed for you." My grandfather's hope that my brother would win the election was put into action as he arranged for the campaign cards to be printed.

Use of any campaign material, such as campaign cards with the candidate's picture on it and with information about the office he was seeking, was unprecedented at my brother's high school. Candidates for school offices had relied on handmade posters which went on walls plus a lot of word-of-mouth efforts asking students for their vote.

My grandfather had been involved in politics for several decades. He knew a lot about how to campaign for elected office. He also had decades of experience as a journalist and as a newspaper publisher. The campaign card was designed, and it was printed at the newspaper where my grandfather was a part-owner. My brother won the election and campaign cards became an essential part of campaigns at that school for many years. My grandfather's hope became action which helped my brother win the election.

When I was quite young, it was apparent that I had a serious speech impediment. For many years I would go to speech therapy and speech training. Progress was made, but the lingering problem of stuttering defied any treatment for years. My grandparents never said anything to me about my speech impediment, but they always included me in conversations. As I recall my impediment was not as extreme when I was at my grandparents' home. What explains that?

In retrospect, the explanation is that they had faith that the speech impediment could be overcome, and they had hope that the speech impediment would be overcome. The hope and the faith were enhanced by action. My grandparents were not trained as speech therapists, but they knew that it was important for me to be included in family discussions so I could begin to see myself as able to speak as well as anyone else. Their caring and loving approach helped. In time, the speech impediment was overcome. Faith and hope, plus much work, prevailed.

My grandparents read many books, news magazines, and newspapers. My grandmother spent much time with her favorite books; although, unless everyone was reading silently, she rarely read while her daughter and her grandsons were visiting because she would have so much to talk about with my mother, my brother, and me. My grandfather also talked with us a lot, yet his decades of experience as a journalist meant that each day he read two or three newspapers. I felt very grown-up when I read a newspaper after he had finished reading it.

Clearly, my grandparents believed that learning could and should continue throughout a person's life. They had much hope that their grandchildren would give reading a high priority. They helped make that happen through occasional gifts of books which resulted in my brother and me eagerly reading then and forever after that. Their belief in the learning that could come through reading helped establish the habit of wholesome reading in my life and no doubt helped lead to advice which I have shared with middle school and high school students for many years: "read, read more, keep reading."

My grandparents believed in life itself. They experienced challenges and complications in their lives, yet they endured, and they prevailed. They were practical people who dealt realistically with challenging situations which did arise, yet they were optimistic people who maintained an inspiring confidence that progress could be made and would be made.

My mother gained her strong sense of hope, faith, and optimism from her parents. Throughout several illnesses, several surgeries, and during her later years as health overall declined, my mother would always say, "I'll feel better tomorrow." She believed that she could feel better tomorrow. She hoped that she would feel better tomorrow. She gave herself that mental advantage of confidently facing challenges. Her parents taught her well and she, in turn, taught her sons well.

Throughout her life, my mother had a strong belief in God. She attended the same Christian church from the time of her college years until her death over 60 years later. She dedicated much time and service to that church. Again, her parents taught her well. She continued that family priority of faith by teaching her sons about faith.

As a child, I did not know the word decorum. If I knew the word decorum when I was a teenager, I doubt that I gave it much attention. As I became a young adult, I must have known the word decorum, but I regret that I gave it little notice.

As an adult in my 60s, I can now realize that my grandparents believed in decorum. They knew that there was a right way to interact with people, that there was a polite way to speak to people, that there was a right way to interact with family members at home, that there was a proper and dignified way to maintain a welcoming, cordial, and polite atmosphere at their home.

As I can realize now, they had faith in abiding by the rules of proper decorum. No doubt, they hoped that their example would be followed by the next generations in our family. They did not establish a dignified decorum at their home to get attention, but to do what they believed was proper, right, and honorable. My mother certainly did learn from her parents about decorum and, as one person said in a perfect description of and tribute to my mother, "She is a most stately lady." I aspire to follow the standard set by my grandparents and confirmed by my mother.

It should be emphasized that the deepest areas of faith which my grandparents lived by were faith in God and faith in each other. They believed strongly in God. They believed strongly in each other. I am certain that those two beliefs overlapped. Part of the action which flowed from their belief in God was to live with a complete dedication to each other in holy matrimony.

Their mutual faith in God was part of the foundation for their belief in each other and their devotion to each other. Their exemplary actions of faith and hope have inspired me throughout my life, inspire me now and always will inspire me. I thank my grandparents for teaching me many life lessons about faith and hope.

Eunice Johnson and Keen Johnson

Judy Babbage and her mother, Eunice Johnson

Keen Babbage, Keen Johnson, Bob Babbage

Eunice Johnson

Keen Johnson, Keen Babbage, Bob Babbage,
Eunice Johnson

Keen Johnson

Keen Johnson

Eunice Johnson

Bob Babbage, Keen Johnson, Keen Babbage at the
opening of Keen Johnson's Lexington, Kentucky 1960
office for the United States
Senate election

Keen Johnson, Bob Babbage

Eunice Johnson, Bob Babbage, Keen Johnson

Keen Johnson, Bob Babbage

Keen Babbage, Eunice Johnson

Keen Johnson

Eunice Johnson

Bob Babbage, Eunice Johnson, Keen Johnson,
Keen Babbage

Bob Babbage, Judy Babbage, Eunice Johnson,
Keen Johnson, Keen Babbage

1960 Keen Johnson for United States Senate
campaign sign

Eunice Johnson, Bob Babbage, Keen Johnson

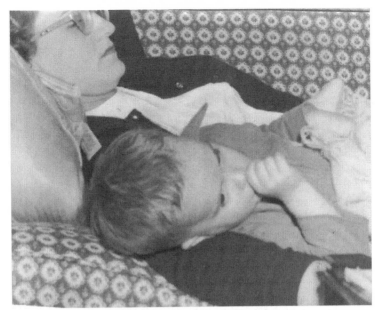

Judy Babbage, Keen Babbage

Judy Babbage

Bob Babbage, Judy Babbage, Keen Babbage

Judy Babbage, Bob Babbage, Keen Babbage in the early
1960's at their Prather Road home in Lexington, Kentucky

Judy Babbage

Judy Babbage

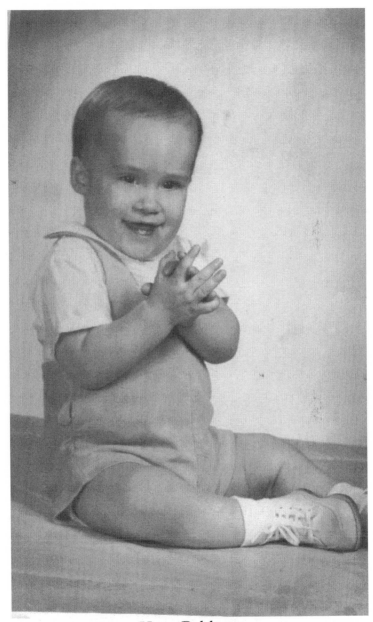

Keen Babbage

Bob Babbage, Keen Babbage

Keen Babbage, Bob Babbage

Keen Babbage

Keen Babbage, Bob Babbage

Keen Babbage with friends

Keen Babbage

Bob Babbage, Keen Babbage

Home at Prather Road in Lexington, Kentucky in the
1960's

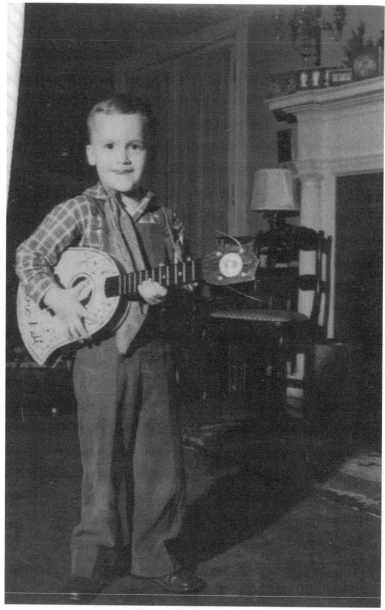

Keen Babbage

5
EDUCATION

At a time when it was unusual to graduate from college, both of my grandparents did exactly that. During his childhood and adolescent years, my grandfather was told by his father that college education was a requirement for Keen Johnson. Why did my great-grandfather think that way?

In the early decades of the 1900's, many jobs were available which did not require any college education. I would suggest that my great-grandfather was thinking of more than the career his son would have; rather, he was also thinking of the overall amount of and quality of knowledge he desired for his son to obtain.

Many, perhaps most, of the conversations I recall sharing with my grandparents from my childhood and teenage years were about what I was doing in school. They were deeply and sincerely interested in the reports I would provide for them about tests I was taking, words I was learning how to spell, math skills I was acquiring, books I was reading, projects I was working on, and daily homework I was doing.

We talked about some of my hobbies and some of my other interests, but the topic of education was given more time and more attention than any other topic. I knew how much it meant to my grandparents to hear that I was doing well in school. Knowing how much my education meant to them gave me an extra reason to take school seriously.

My grandparents reared my mother with the same emphasis on education. My mother once told me about a college professor who told her that at the middle of a semester she had a grade of 'C' in his class. The truth was that she had a grade of 'A' in the class, but the professor thought he was being clever and amusing to suggest that she was doing average work.

Her response to the statement of the professor was to double her effort in the class. She earned an 'A' for the class which was the grade she had all along. Why did she double her effort to ensure that her grade would be an 'A'? When I asked her about that she answered that question with these words: "I knew how much it meant to my parents that I make an 'A' in every class."

At the University of Kentucky, my mother earned an 'A' in every class she took during her four years as a college student. She became a member of Phi Beta Kappa. She learned much. Her achievements pleased her, but knowing how much those accomplishments pleased her parents was the greatest reward for her for all her determined academic work.

It meant much to me during my years in junior high school, as we called middle school back then, and in high school to be able to tell my parents and my grandparents that I had made the honor roll at school. They truly celebrated with smiles, hugs, and cheers. I knew that their love for me was not dependent on my grades in school, but I knew that getting good grades in school was a way for me to express my love for them and my appreciation for them.

Their encouragement for me to do well in school was part of their expression of love for me. My determination to do well in school was part of my expression of love for them. As I think upon those times now, it is obvious that everyone benefitted from the encouraging, loving, and supportive bond we had.

Muny and Paw-Wah used to ask me questions whenever we were together. They were eager to know what I was learning in school. I must have thought that if those topics were important to them that I should be sure those topics were important to me. Because they asked me about school so often, I had to be sure that there was always some good news to tell them about excellent grades and wholesome experiences at school.

From their perspective, I deserved their encouragement and support. From my perspective, they deserved to hear that I was working hard and accomplishing a lot. Because my grandparents gave education such a high priority and because they taught my mother to give her education a high priority, I got the same message. No doubt, that encouragement, support, and priority were factors in my decision to become a teacher.

My grandparents helped me understand that education should continue throughout the year, including the months when school was not in session. During the summer I would sometimes spend several consecutive days with my grandparents. Those days were filled with projects to do around their home. I would help with tasks I was given. While the tasks were being done, I would ask many questions.

Where had my grandparents lived before they moved into the only house I knew that they had called home? Why had they moved several times? Why did they move from Elizabethtown, Kentucky to Lawrenceburg, Kentucky before settling and staying in Richmond, Kentucky? What was it like to work at a newspaper? How was Missouri – my grandmother's place of birth – different from Kentucky?

These discussions prompted me to learn more. My grandparents would share pictures with me about places where they had lived and where they had traveled. Those pictures increased my eagerness to know more and that took me to the encyclopedia. I would look up topic after topic and read everything that early version of a search engine could tell me. After summer experiences which were enjoyable and educational, I would return to school with excitement about recently learned ideas and with newly acquired information. Summer learning prepared me well for each new school year.

My grandfather's words from a 1941 commencement speech he gave at Eastern Kentucky State Teachers College, a regional, state-supported Kentucky college which later became Eastern Kentucky University, shows the value my grandfather placed on education while also showing the responsibility he knew that education placed on people who had learned much.

"Has this education which you have obtained during these years in which you have been going to school developed in you a finer appreciation of moral values? Do you not only demand the precious freedoms guaranteed under the Constitution, such as the freedom of the press, of speech, of religious worship, of assembly, and all other freedoms set forth in the Bill of Rights, but do you also appreciate the fact that there is resting upon you corresponding duties and responsibilities to be a good citizen?

"Has your education developed in you a keener appreciation of honesty in your dealings with your fellowman and in those transactions which you have with the state? Do you believe in justice and righteousness, and will you work to see that they prevail? Are you interested in giving as well as getting? Are you conscious of the dignity of every personality and that the individual counts regardless of his station in life? If you have sentiments like these in your heart, the state has made a good investment in you." (The Public Papers of Governor Keen Johnson; published in 1982 by the University Press of Kentucky; page 155)

I have a copy of Thomas Merton's masterpiece, "The Seven Storey Mountain." The book has a 1948 copyright. In addition to the deep insights and earnest yearnings presented by the author, this book brings to me an additional meaning. How does Merton's book do that? Because in the front of the book, in her artistic handwriting, my grandmother wrote "Eunice N. Johnson, July 1949."

I acquired this book in the year 2016 from a person whom I met at a banquet. During the dinner conversation, the gentleman realized that Mrs. Johnson was my grandmother and that he had a book in which she had signed her name. He was not certain about how he had acquired the book, but he was certain that the book should be given to me. It is a gift which is deeply appreciated.

I read "The Seven Storey Mountain" immediately after I was given that book. It was not the author who spoke to me through his wisdom that mattered most to me, although the book truly is a magnificent literary and intellectual achievement. What mattered most to me was that I was reading the exact book which my grandmother had read in 1949. I could imagine how she reacted to the ideas of the book.

Because my grandmother read that book, I was given the opportunity to read that book. Because she learned from that book, I was given the opportunity to learn from that book. On an intellectual level, reading that book enhanced my knowledge of Thomas Merton's journey of faith. On a personal level, reading that book enhanced my knowledge of my grandmother. She read that book to add to her ongoing education. When I read her copy of that book, my ongoing education was enhanced, and our already very strong family bond was strengthened.

Keen Johnson and Eunice Johnson valued education. Through their example and because of their encouragement, I have placed a very high priority on education throughout my life, including working in middle schools and in high schools for 34 years. I have advised students throughout the years to "learn, learn more, keep learning."

I used to think that I had created that statement which I shared with my students. Instead, I shared with my students what my grandparents shared with me. Their commitment to and their appreciation of education continues to have an impact. As I type this paragraph I am pausing for a moment to applaud my grandparents and to say anew a word of deeply felt thanks for them, of respect for them, and of love for them.

6
MANNERS

"What happened? What went wrong? When did so much change? Why did so much change? Do people realize what has been lost? Does it concern people that behavior which was once absolutely unacceptable has become common and apparently approved?

"Why do people in music and in television programs and in movies use such crude and vulgar language? Why do music and television programs and movies treat immorality as if it is expected that most people will do what is wrong and never think of it as wrong?

"Where did standards of right and wrong go? What happened to being polite? When did children and teenagers start calling an adult by the adult's first name? When did so many students at school become disrespectful of adults at school and disobedient toward adults at school?

"When did some people in public office start using vulgar language regularly in their speeches and why do voters vote for such people? When was it decided that political disagreements must include vicious name calling and harsh personal accusations instead of having a sensible, civil discussion of ideas within boundaries of competition?

"What happened to 'Yes, sir' and 'No, ma'am?' What happened to the automatic respect which goes with how children and teenagers should speak to and act toward adults?

"Do people say please when they should? Do people say thank you when they should? Are people who run businesses polite to their customers? There seems to be so much less decency in how people treat each other. What happened? What went wrong?

"Do people realize that these mistakes must be corrected and that proper standards do not change even if behaviors change or decline at certain times?

We can do better. Can we all commit to do better? Can we all commit to a dedication to proper standards? Please, do not lower standards to match a decline in behavior. Instead, improve the behavior to match the proper standards which served people so well for so long."

Those questions could very reasonably and very seriously be asked to show the concern of and the perspective of a person from my grandparents' generation to people of today. What would the answers be?

My grandparents were mannerly, polite, properly behaved, respectable, and gracious people. These characteristics were not ways of thinking or ways of behaving which they forced on themselves; rather, these characteristics were essential parts of who they were. My grandparents saw no option other than to be polite.

Being polite was not one possibility of how a person might live or how a person might treat others. For my grandparents, being polite was part of their character, of their integrity, and was part of the set of standards they required themselves to live by. They were not polite to impress people. They were polite because they each knew that being a person of good manners is right. It's just right.

I am at my best when I follow the standards of being polite and mannerly which my grandparents lived by. Upon decades of reflection, I am convinced that my grandparents thought of being polite as part of the proper ethical and moral standards to live by.

For them, there were not situations when a person was to be polite and other situations when a person could be rude. Having good manners was part of being a good person and that was not negotiable, not variable, and not occasional. My grandparents did not view good manners and being polite as restrictions which were imposed on them; rather, having good manners and being polite were important parts of how they lived, of who they were, of what they valued, and of what they understood was honorable. Consider these examples:

When I was 10 years old I spent a week attending a church summer camp. My mother purchased some postcards for me, so I could write to my grandparents and tell them about camp. I had not thought of writing to my family as part of the activities of camp, but I quickly learned that those postcards meant a lot to my grandparents.

Rather than be out of touch with my grandparents for a week, the polite and proper action to take was to send them postcards with information about camp. My mother taught me about that. In a time when long distance phone calls were expensive, writing postcards was a good way to continue a long family tradition of being in touch by mail whenever travel caused a brief separation.

Yes, these traditions of postcard writing, or letter writing, were parts of an era prior to cell phones, text messages, and e-mail. The emphasis was not on the form of communication, although postcards were convenient and were common then. The emphasis was on thinking of other people and politely communicating with them.

My grandparents attended separate colleges in Missouri. They occasionally saw each other, but those in-person times were limited. Between visits, they wrote letters to each other. The letters were kind, considerate, and very proper. The letters confirmed a growing mutual interest and fondness, but such thoughts were always expressed within boundaries of proper social standards and within good manners.

As a child it was my good fortune to attend public events with my parents and with my grandparents. I noticed that my grandfather always held a door open for my grandmother, my mother, and my father, plus for my brother and me. As I grew old enough to do that task, it meant a lot to me that I could hold a door open for my family. Following my grandfather's example meant that I was learning about good manners from an expert.

I further noticed that when we were being seated at a table for a meal that my grandfather would make sure that my grandmother was seated before he sat down. He would help her with her chair. As a child I probably wondered why my grandmother needed someone to pull out her chair and then help push it back in toward the table. My grandmother could have moved the chair.

I later realized that there was something more to this than the physical movement of a chair. There was the expression of consideration and of manners which matched my grandfather's upbringing, and which matched the social norm of the times. If those norms have changed it would be reasonable to ask why and to ask what impact the changes have had.

The next-door neighbors of my grandparents built a swimming pool in their back yard. These neighbors welcomed the entire neighborhood to use the pool. Whenever my brother and I would swim there, Muny would ask us, upon our return to her home, if we had thanked the neighbors for letting us swim. If there was ever any doubt, we would go back to speak to the neighbors and express our appreciation.

There were times when Paw-Wah would take me to see the offices and other facilities of the newspaper which he co-owned. The actions of the printing press fascinated me. I noticed that my grandfather spoke to everyone at the newspaper. The workers there knew that he was one of the owners of the newspaper, and they were respectful toward him. He often took the initiative and spoke to people letting them know that he appreciated their work. It was polite to speak to the workers. It was also good business management.

On Mother's Day, we went with Muny to her church. On Father's Day, we went with Paw-Wah to his church. Those two churches were across the street from each other. It intrigued me that my grandparents attended separate churches, but that was out of a mutual respect for the unique and individual heritage which they each had as it related to faith.

When I was 13 years old and my brother was 16 years old, we spent a few days with our grandfather while our grandmother had to be out of town. One evening we went to a restaurant for supper. The restaurant was part of a group of about 50 locations that a Kentucky-owned company had throughout the state. There was nothing fancy about the restaurant. It was a pleasant, family-friendly, comfortable place with good food.

What I recall from supper at that restaurant was how my grandfather spoke with the waitress. My grandfather had known presidents of companies and presidents of the United States. He had travelled the nation and the world. Yet, at this one local restaurant he gave much attention to the good work which our waitress did. He thanked her for the excellent effort and the very good service she provided.

I remember that she smiled when she heard the compliment. She seemed to be very encouraged and to be a bit surprised. Perhaps she was having a demanding day or perhaps customers were not often appreciative. My grandfather's good manners brought a moment of kindness to that hard-working waitress.

One of the life lessons which my grandparents' example of good manners and of being polite continues to teach me is that some standards of behavior are inherently right and should not change over time. It is still right to be polite and to have good manners. That standard has not changed, and that standard should not change. To the extent that our society has drifted from good manners and from being polite, a return to the proper standard of an earlier generation would be wholesome, smart, beneficial, and proper.

The burden of proof is on those who would say that lower standards are preferred. The benefits of higher standards, of good manners and of being polite are, to borrow Thomas Jefferson's words about certain rights of people as he expressed that idea in the Declaration of Independence, "self-evident." My grandparents just knew that being polite and having good manners were inherently right. They were correct about that then, and they are forever correct about that.

7

"SAVING, THRIFTY, FRUGAL"

The words cited below were spoken by Governor Keen Johnson on September 6, 1940 in Wilmore, Kentucky. The audience was composed of people attending the Kentucky Methodist Church Conference.

"There are times when political associates become exasperated because of my refusal to sanction expenditures of public money which they regard as desirable. I acquired the habit of saving and thrifty in a humble Methodist parsonage where such was a necessity. I was taught to avoid wastefulness. Extravagance was held up to be a sin and I so regard it, regardless of whether it be in the expenditure of public money or private funds.

"And I was never more sincere in my life than when as a candidate, I promised the people that I would make a saving, thrifty, frugal governor. The characteristic which results in me placing such emphasis upon that philosophy of public expenditure is the direct result of having been reared in a humble Methodist parsonage." (The Public Papers of Governor Keen Johnson 1939-1943; published in 1982 by the University Press of Kentucky; page 437)

Governor Johnson kept his promise to be "saving, thrifty, and frugal" during his years as governor of Kentucky. During the years of 1935-1939 when Keen Johnson served as Kentucky's Lieutenant Governor and worked with Governor "Happy" Chandler and then during the years 1939-1943 when Keen Johnson served as Kentucky's Governor, the state went from having a financial deficit to having a financial surplus. "Saving, thrifty, and frugal" got good results.

I vividly recall a Saturday afternoon when Paw-Wah took me to downtown Richmond, Kentucky. There were several places to stop, including the newspaper he co-owned and which, in his retirement years, he

59

continued to write editorials for.

We walked by a record shop and I asked if we could go in. My grandfather agreed, but I could tell that he was not very interested in this store. There was one record which had my favorite song on it. It was one of those temporarily popular songs which can capture the attention of a young person. I asked my grandfather if he would buy the record for me. The price was one dollar.

My grandfather made it clear to me that he did not see how the record could be worth one dollar. He knew that the song would be forgotten soon and that the record would be used for a few days and then never played again. He reluctantly purchased the record for me. I was thrilled to have a record with my favorite song.

His unspoken prediction soon came true. The record got my attention for a few days and then it was put aside as new interests developed. The dollar had been wasted. A lesson had been learned: there is an important difference between what we want and what we need. I wanted the record. I did not need the record.

During my grandfather's career, he often travelled by train for business trips. For various vacations, my grandparents traveled by train. Passenger train usage was still quite prominent during much of their lifetimes.

The story is told of a time when my grandfather had lunch in the dining car of a passenger train. The bill for lunch was $1.40 and my grandfather gave the waiter two dollars. The change would be brought promptly.

The waiter did some thinking. Should he make the change as two quarters and one dime? Should he make the change as one dime and one half-dollar coin (half dollar coins were common at that time)? If he returned the two quarters and one dime, it is likely that his tip would have been a quarter. If he returned one half-dollar coin and a dime, he hoped that his tip would be the half-dollar, but that was uncertain. The waiter decided to take his chances with the dime and the half-dollar coin.

When the change was returned to my grandfather on a small tray, Paw-Wah immediately picked up the half-dollar coin and put it in his pocket. He left the dime as the tip. The waiter quickly and very politely said, "That's all right, Governor. That's all right. I gambled and lost." If the waiter had known how important it was to my grandfather to be "saving, thrifty, and frugal," he would have known not to gamble with the change arrangement.

When Keen Johnson became Governor of Kentucky in 1939, there was some printed stationery left over from his predecessor, Governor Chandler. Of course, the available stationery had the name of Governor Chandler on it. Keen Johnson did not immediately order that new stationery be printed with his name on it; rather, he used the available stationery and simply put a line through his predecessor's name and wrote in his own name. Anyone who received formal communication from Governor Johnson could easily see what he had done with the stationery and could quickly realize that he would save money for Kentucky whenever possible.

My grandmother showed us a good example of being thrifty one year on the day after Thanksgiving. Our family's holiday meal on Thanksgiving had included turkey. Our family's main meal on the day after Thanksgiving featured turkey hash. When we were told that the main dish for the meal would be turkey hash, my brother and I did not know what to expect. When the turkey hash was being prepared, we understood that no turkey meat would go to waste. The turkey hash was absolutely delicious and the thriftiness to fully use the turkey for more than one meal was noticed.

It became obvious to me that nothing was wasted in my grandmother's kitchen. She planned meals precisely knowing what food to have and how much of it to have. Any leftovers were seen as the beginning of another meal.

There was a family-owned grocery store in Richmond, Kentucky which would deliver groceries to customers. Muny would call them to place an order. Her order was completely thought out. She knew how much of everything would be needed.

I sometimes heard her part of the conversation when she was on the phone with someone at the grocery store. She would read from her carefully prepared grocery list. That type of household management was a clear example of emphasizing needs over wants, of emphasizing control and of avoiding extravagance.

My grandfather was reared in a humble home where the budget was always tight. My grandmother's father died when she was nine months old, so her family had to carefully manage their budget. They both learned the importance of saving, of being thrifty, of being frugal.

Years of living within well-managed financial budgets and boundaries eventually enabled Muny and Paw-Wah to live a comfortable lifestyle. Still, they always remained true to what they knew to be right about managing family resources. Their standard is summarized in three words: saving, thrifty, frugal. Their standard teaches a very helpful life lesson.

EPILOGUE
POLITICS AND MORE

In 1960, Keen Johnson was the Kentucky Democrat party candidate for the United States Senate. I was six years old then and my brother, Bob, was nine years old. Bob and I walked house-to-house through part of our neighborhood distributing brochures for our grandfather to help in his campaign. We excitedly watched a televised debate between our grandfather and his Republican opponent.

On election night my brother and I were convinced that our grandfather would win. We watched some news on television and what we saw seemed favorable to us. I remember chanting, "Paw-Wah's gonna win. Paw-Wah's gonna win." That victorious result did not occur. Still, my brother and I learned much about politics from our grandfather.

The interest in and the many achievements in public service, in government, in politics which Bob has had for many years began in our childhood and were manifested in adulthood. Bob has served in several elected positions: as a member of the Lexington, Kentucky city council, as Kentucky's State Auditor and as Kentucky's Secretary of State. He then became a very accomplished and respected lobbyist. My interest in studying about and later in teaching the topics of history and government also had a foundation in the childhood years.

Keen Johnson was an acclaimed journalist in Kentucky during the 1920's and 1930's. This was a time when a newspaper had a strong support for one major political party and a strong opposition to the other major political party. The editorial perspective of the three newspapers which Keen Johnson invested in was decidedly in favor of the Democrat party. The many editorials he wrote in those newspapers earned recognition from journalists throughout Kentucky and from Democrat political leaders in Kentucky.

He remained involved in journalism throughout his adult life, but in the 1930's he made a transition to significant involvement in politics. He became an official in and an employee of the Kentucky Democrat party. His work with people throughout Kentucky as a journalist and as a Democrat Party official created a base of support which resulted in him being encouraged by many friends and colleagues to seek public office.

In 1935, Keen Johnson was elected as Lieutenant Governor of Kentucky, and in 1939, he was elected to be the Governor of Kentucky. After leaving the office of Governor, he had a long career in public relations with the Reynolds Metals Company until his retirement in 1961. Also, he served for one year at President Truman's request as the Under-Secretary of Labor.

The following statements are from speeches given by Keen Johnson. Those speeches and many other Johnson documents were compiled in "The Public Papers of Governor Keen Johnson" which was published in 1982 by the University Press of Kentucky.

There are life lessons, insights, ideas, challenges, calls to action, and words of wisdom in the following statements. For now, let's give ourselves the opportunity to travel back to the 1930's and 1940's to learn from words spoken then by Governor Keen Johnson.

"I am grateful to so many of you as voted for me, for having given me this opportunity to serve all of you as your governor. I shall try to justify your confidence by diligently endeavoring to make you a saving, thrifty, frugal governor." (page 6)

"I will not make you a spectacular governor, but I will try harder than did any of my predecessors to make you a good, honest governor." (page 6)

"I hope that there may be a wider acceptance of the fact that the best politics is good government and that politics reaches its highest justification as it advances better government." (page 8)

"It is our good fortune to live within a great and beautiful state, peopled by a splendid, intelligent, patriotic citizenship. I would not feel fit to be your governor if I did not feel a great love for Kentucky and her people. Love for Kentucky is with me a holy passion." (page 8)

"There is no more effective program of national defense than to prepare the youth of each generation to face a crisis calmly, discharge the duties of citizenship under stress of war, or intelligently analyze the problems of peace and find sane solutions for them. Adequate preparation of the younger generation for civic duty is vital to the perpetuity of this nation." (page 124)

"No easy shortcut to an education has yet been discovered. Great as has been the progress in the science of teaching, prolonged, sustained mental effort is still necessary in getting an education. There have been many labor-saving devices perfected. But no invention has yet been stricken off by the brain of man which reduces the mental exertion necessary to reach the goal of graduation." (page 135)

"The world will never change so much that the old virtues will not remain the yardstick by which we measure character. Honesty and courage, vision and intelligence, thoroughness and integrity are qualities you may cultivate without fear that a changing world will render them obsolete." (page 140)

"To learn how to read to save their souls was the first great urge that caused many to secure the fundamentals of an education. With the founding of the republic, it became evident to the leaders that people should learn how to read and think to save their independence and freedom." (page 153)

"In that parsonage in which I spent my childhood, the family altar was a sacred shrine at which the family worshiped each evening. Family prayer was held each morning at breakfast. At evening prayer, father prayed first. He seemed to feel that he was talking directly to the God in whom he had implicit faith. He gave Him a lot of advice, asked Him for many things he never got. But that did not alter his belief in the God he worshiped. His explanation of the failure of those blessings to arrive for which he had petitioned was that God knew such would not be best." (page 438)

"I am beginning to wonder if it is not perhaps true that we have depended too much on education to reduce crime and banish war. I wonder if it is not probable that we have placed too great emphasis upon the development of the mental process and neglected that spiritual development of the finer impulses of the human heart." (page 441)

"Mother love is the most sublime of human emotions. The love of mother for her children is tender, compassionate, as enduring as it is strong. It is expressed in daily devotion in which mother expends herself in behalf of her children."(page 475)

The lives of, the work of, the examples of, the standards of, and the priorities of Keen Johnson and Eunice Johnson provide life lessons with value beyond measure. To learn from them is to learn about what is right, what is true, what is honorable, and what matters most. Muny and Paw-Wah taught their family members very well. The wisdom of Keen Johnson and Eunice Johnson endures, now and forever.

ABOUT THE AUTHOR

Keen Babbage, Ed. D., retired from a 27-year career in public education in 2016. He had been a middle school teacher, a middle school assistant principal, and a high school teacher. Earlier and later in his career, he worked for seven years at three private schools. He has also worked in advertising/marketing for eight years at three large companies.

He has written 22 books about education with emphasis on two areas: teaching, and school leadership/management. He has written three additional books: *Life Lessons from Cancer* (co-authored by Laura Babbage); *Life Lessons from a Dog Named Rudy*; and *Take More Naps*. He lives in Lexington, Kentucky.

Made in the USA
Middletown, DE
17 February 2021